DAUGHTER OF THE HANGNAIL

The New Issues Press Poetry Series

Editor	Herbert Scott
Advisory Editors	Nancy Eimers, Mark Halliday William Olsen, J. Allyn Rosser
Assistant to the Editor	Rebecca Beech
Assistant Editors	Allegra Blake, Jenny Burkholder, Becky Cooper, Rita Howe Scheiss, Nancy Hall James, Kathleen McGookey, Tony Spicer
Editorial Assistants	Melanie Finlay, Pamela McComas
Business Manager	Michele McLaughlin
Fiscal Officer	Marilyn Rowe

The New Issues Press Poetry Series is sponsored by The College of Arts and Sciences, Western Michigan University.

First Edition, 1997.

ISBN: 0-932826-56-3 (cloth)
ISBN: 0-932826-57-1 (paper)

Library of Congress Cataloging-in-Publication Data:
Reynolds, Rebecca 1962–
Rebecca Reynolds/Daugher of the Hangnail
Library of Congress Catalog Card Number 97-67321

Art Direction:	Tricia Hennessy
Design:	Cris Logan
Production:	Paul Sizer
	The Design Center, Department of Art
	Western Michigan University
Printing:	Bookcrafters, Chelsea, Michigan

DAUGHTER OF THE HANGNAIL

REBECCA REYNOLDS

FOREWORD BY MARY RUEFLE

New Issues Press

WESTERN MICHIGAN UNIVERSITY

To Miranda
in memory of Leon and Pauline

My heart is breaking for a little love.
While bee-hives wake and whir
And rabbit thins his fur . . .
—Christina Rossetti

Contents

III

Foreword

Any encounter with a talented new poet is a thrill, and a visceral one, because he or she is so freshly drunk on language, so utterly lost in looking. If that is so, Rebecca Reynolds is soused. At the same time, the old-new thrills give way (and make way) for something else, a sober and ripening intelligence that each generation recasts in its own image. Rilke's famous words—call them a definition—he was a poet and hated the approximate (also translated he was a poet; he loathed the inexact) have fallen on hard times. What does it mean to be exact when the world is full of aberration? When the very notion of exactness is constantly challenged by shifting perspective? "Each word, glued with unending multiplications of the aberrant—" Reynolds says in one poem, and the inquisitive, the parenthetical, the word or, all serve this poet in deciphering flux and sniffing deception, not with indifference—never that—but with wonder, the tactile wonder that never leaves her and leaves her poems so richly textured and deeply felt. These poems develop, as all things do, by dividing and reassembling in new ways. The self likewise unfolds ("the earlier self/ postmarked without promise of arrival"); the poet in these poems is not finding herself (what a relief!) but making herself; if she is "lost in a world of resemblances," a world without harmony or implication, it is with a sense of the endlessness of the human capacity for questions, the endlessness of self-making that is therefore full of possibility, a hopefulness I think she alludes to when she says "the crumbs that Gretel/ scatters on the stumps are not for her/ to find her way back but for others". These poems move bravely forward and conjure the mood of a long Stevensian walk through a post-industrial town at twilight, a town that has seen better times, a town full of houses and apartments where people can be seen in lit rooms, gathered around tables and televisions, trying in very different ways to collate their experience after a day of labor. When Reynolds—whose daring labor is language— asks "Is it possible to peel/ eternal questions from the alphabet" she has just done so, since that is, in itself, an eternal question. The book is full of— dare I say it?— eternal questions, and if we are reminded poetry is a good house in a bad neighborhood, making beauty a logistical error, we are also made aware it has stood there for a very long time and is in no danger of falling down or being torn down, so long as poets like Reynolds are given stewardship of this strange conundrum called poetry. But I have said too much; the best introduction to a new poet is the work itself.

Mary Ruefle

Acknowledgements

Poems in this book have previously appeared in:

Caliban: "Blue Shift" (as "Testing Perspectives")

US1 Worksheets: "Peridot"

Earth's Daughters: "The Ample House"

Blue Violin: "A Small Business"

Third Coast: "The Pole-Vaulter"

American Letters and Commentary: "Anatomy of a Beast" and "Sequence in Lime"

Grateful acknowledgement is made to the New Jersey Arts Council for a fellowship that enabled me to work on this book. I also wish to acknowledge Mark Richardson and Ruth Yeselson for their patience and support, and my teachers, past and present.

I

In the world's structure dream
loosens individuality like a bad tooth.

—Walter Benjamin

The Pole-Vaulter

Perhaps nothing is not a surface: a red tea,
nectarines dozing in a green bowl,

the house ruffled in a single breath
with National Public Radio in its cells.

Say that space were the only variable. A road
snakes out of the Holland tunnel, and so on

through the Catskills' miles-to-go-before-I-sleep
in fore-schemes of brick, begonia,

and later, that immense shale.
Back here, a carcass of whiting lies on the table.

Bones open it, like pins stuck in yellowed, antique crepe
in the slice of work/home/work. The past

is headless, like a fine stem. Of course,
the steadily awake are still

curling thick fingers around the bone-white cups
in a 24-hour coffee shop. By "bone," I mean "imperfect."

Because we're stuck
between being here and not being here, although

the only thing beyond me is a point:
the lamp or the particular star

pinned to the felt in Lucy Osborne's diorama
of the birth of Christ, circa 1968. And my half-Jewish heart

starved for the only child. His only duty—
to be loved. And look:

the viridian dusk may still be distinguished
over the fresh headstones of a village.

The Man who Kept Birds

Man discovered with over 700 birds in his apartment

Man, single, loves animals.
To lure the remotest speck from its light path: birds,
wooed from the trees,
triple x marquees, atop

houses of love. Until the inside was alien
and the outside, in.
Legs of ingested berry, white liner notes—
these were the effluence.

And in the end, the finches had whipped the kitchen
into a hatch. Of course
that didn't bother him,
but if you're asking whether the birds themselves had gotten
     sardonic,

he couldn't fathom, even if there was something
to their high oblivion. Or the seeds,
jetsamed in red gruel. In fact
he cherished these small frights.

The pecking order,
fervid knots of starlings,
and his poor head, startled,
the way a floorplan is startled with wings.

"Crazy bastard," we thought.
It was an epithet he knew;
affected by plumage in the shift
from girls to gulls.

A simple displacement, supple,
as in a dream, in which you rescue, tenderly,

some lover who jilted you.
But why is her head hurt? Why is she limping?

Was it vanity
to claim her, like a corner-piece of the unknown,
to tap life in the beating surface?
Can you get *life* from *life*,

if we receive but what we give?
For though the seed-cake was no longer so finely apportioned,
the birds had returned.
There might have been some grand design

before the neighbors came
with the TV crew, the Animal Rescue League,
the police, the fire chief,
and the landlady.

Only the topic we instantly recognized:
man finds solace
bringing the world inside.
Feather-skin, minute wish-bones,

flashmaps in the brain,
or what he could have of the world.

Anatomy of a Beast

> *About him lay the carcasses of many several beasts newly*
> *by him cut-up and anatomized; not that he did contemn*
> *God's creatures as he told Hippocrates, but to find out*
> *the seat of the atra bilis, or melancholy . . .*
> —-Burton, The Anatomy of Melancholy

i.
You can't infer emotion from the eyes
when light moves neither in nor out.

What he sensed was oblivion. The mouth, grim,
reposing in a blue frown, a bone

left by the laurel, a frayed nerve—
and the investigator returned

to his dark life.

ii.
She begins to understand her body as event,
its green matrix on screen

a pivoting system of open rungs
fluctuating between

beauty, and not beauty. Change the structure.
It's like someone standing at the top of the stairs

looking oh so far down at her.
In the electronic medium, she discovers

translucence, what she is.

iii.
Of course, he's seen it all. Love
evaporating like ice, when spring persists

remarkably around the windows, and Melancholy
walks on water. It's not explicit

from whence it comes, how long it lasts,
why he pores over meticulous illustration, the flesh

he wants to open—to discover in the red flash of meaning
his body. Instead,

the lamp scouts a hole above his slack material.
The housekeeper pads in and out with meat, her feet

crossing, and re-crossing. Outside, the beast
is quietly cut up. There is no novelty here.

If the beast is human, the experiment is our grief.

Range Finder

Thin phenomena that air disperses.
The event,

the driving incident, before
becoming part of the story: *my fat father,*

the wedding dress,
the group doing the mazurka in a damp hall,

the hint of pork and blue laws.
Until the surfaces inhere, or a shape

resembles itself. Something large
reduced to time and space, for the purposes

of being small. And the story
forges a pursuit. Steady

as the light in the night air that would take me
pole-wards, because I wanted to keep north

and discover plains, where the snow was like felt—
and the far-off stammer of houses

in their blonde wood. Otherwise
I thought of glimpsing what was wholly inside:

a woman trying to talk about herself,
to map the spareness of discovery. A separateness in which

I am not *true*, but approximate, containing sight
and distance

which is all I have between touch.

The Object of Burial is Intent

Accretion,
      dispossession

in the parlor of breath. A thing
refuses to resonate (I'm thinking
of the object lost from its threads)

as if I could make it signify
"in the beginning" despite
this death-log of nature. Not like this—

when something you love turns to this dialogue
between birth and death:
in the beginning was the end—

and in the end, the starship
stumbling on this loop between
past and future

infinitely repairs
its history. To alter
so no alteration finds.

And here I was digging and undigging
to fix an awkwardness, a clutter
      that runs in the genes

like diabetes or mood swings;
why the self
is a description of the body,

why we must hope
that love is blind:
so that someone will take us.

The Naïve Bones

The imagery I devised:

two thin, looping flowers
with small cross-hatchings on the skin
in the assigned colors. The aspirants

in pairs, took light
from the top.

      *

Two round loping stones
on the scenic side, sat
against the valley. Looking over my mother said,

"it's either Connecticut or Massachusetts."

The feathery miles, the overlook,
my dress, a certain Aztec resolution
gone red. Something,

someone, is fathered.

                 Farther,
glinting, ruled, rudish,
a wheel of air, a loop

boarding the *Lythrum* and joe-pye,
accidentally small on the floor
of the distance—

      a multitude

      *

as a certain red
has no orientation.
What was rooted in flesh

like an infirmity:
my blue skin,
the inner thump and lag

of a feeling—
other aspirations/breath
        between the bones

and obscurity (I was light

intercepted). While she lived
in that foreground of local stone,

a frequency
        fixed in the complex,
where a solid

        defines space, and a gully

expounds.

            *

A frequency ignites
like the angels' bodies,

        Igneous and Lucid
over the colonies.

Thirty Storms

Knife. Unsayable

when the impenetrability would be consistent

with a more experimental voice

and the air drops

even further below what we would call zero, the surface
    of a light

substance   houses that blink in ice

resemble a series of chalets (but where

is the alp?) she sits

by the knife and the cyclamen\the quiet phone

a lamp that writes.   the flowers

have been tending her all winter   I mean "marcescent"

the flower unfolds and unfolds

    a thread that crosses under cloud

in the composition of detail unless

through   she may open the circle to intake
     entering

a center of grease and cigarette ash (magical realism)

A white leg falls in the white snow. A white arm

how this body and that body, somewhere

the sycamore grow

    worn and flawed   the color of bottle glass

(a hospital of color)

Consider dyeing a dress wintergreen, like a mint

at the bottom of your heart.

    I hate to see the petals unfurl like ears

but there is nothing for the word—   for this   (   )

is the first line.I have longed for an infinite dialogue

Sarah's Foot

> *But his wife looked back behind him*
> *and she became a pillar of salt.*

i.
The vetch, the stone, the red sand on the path,
the citizen's arrest—
        that removal from love
the moment she became an outlaw. One day
she slipped into self-help, mingled
among the Jesus-with-the-bleeding-hearts
against a green wall. It was the cloth
she adored, the meeting rooms
stiff with coats, the wool on her palm, the clothes
in which her body cohered; her body
and His wound, luminous and enforced,
                where a cut became
de rigueur
though she had no faith. Significance
grew smaller and pin-like.
She loused the IQ
(couldn't describe a nail
or say Columbus discovered America)
as if she'd flown on a sad vacation, without
communicants. Enter the new year,
rubbed and startling in its thinness. The paths
would lead to no
ultimatums, recoveries,
or even lenience. She noted dresses
on passing women. How emptily they hung
because of all the air surrounding.

ii.
Lamps pretended to be stones, pretended
to be lamps. Words were like driftwood,
bleached and smooth
without the tendency of a grain
until she was hungry for apparency or a room
battened with humans.
This is how the librarian packs the houses back on the shelves,
shuts the windows in the books
and kisses the eyes of the sleepers, marveling
at their pint-sized brains. If only she could be closed
or unitary, she could say
I am here, or walking on the tree farm, or
ahead in my father's gray Ford,
(though she could be elsewhere).
She would need a world
without the luxuries of fiction
where a world springs up. There is less
she can touch now
that isn't technical and reluctant.
Even the young Jane Eyre
had Helen Burns; her incumbent faith,
her inhuman love.

iii.
The earth is one long episode.
Describe a shift: a shift
is a dull pain, like a hill. Also
a nail, which I mis-described,
like a deputy with keys to the jailhouse
that never opens or closes; and unbeknownst to him
the gang is at the barber's, and it's perpetual light.
Take one shift with a bromide, then call—
lest the hedges become salt, lest
one of us becomes salt
though I'd prefer salt
to no following, lest I
am singular, the breath
stuck in a receiver without
reception (except the TV) in an empty house, the breath
flexed and hung
with the rude flowers or sit-com. And
noting the comedy of human sorrow
I'd take a dim view of this depression.
Though faith, too, is obscure:
I don't remember why the bush burned
or why its burning was remarked (oh yes
now I do). Things comes back
in the smallest pieces.

iv.
I didn't always get the hang of love, though perhaps
I knew it, as we know the tick of winter
in the bleached wind, or the wire's stutter over the roof
when the cat curls under the lamp, and the color of milk
becomes pink
lapping in snow. I also
missed the question about Columbus
or how to put two squares together to form
the inside of a box. I kept saying "open a side,"
but we were supposed to do it without that direction.
And I've wondered whether Jane was happy in the end,
after all, it didn't suit her, that sudden
upper-hand; nor could I be your eyes.
Once we scoured the landscape for a pair of pants
that had flown off the hotel balcony
into a ravine of goats. It was
January in the south of Spain that year and
I was there.

Dragging the Riverbeds

The latest crime in America
is the carjacking of women.

I believe only in lines, midnight's
dispersal of bodies along the lines

they meant to travel, along the lines
of trees. Our witnesses, asleep.

And we, here, are bluer than before, lonelier
than a body of water, than the middle of the night.

She lived alone in a state filled with wheat and apples
amid tarnished cowbells, the buff rocks

of her state, in the middle
of a country—

Don't ask where the women go,
why the fiancés are dragging the riverbeds,

Detroit up in arms
about bad press. My friend says

she got sideswiped on 94,
says someone did it on purpose.

Later, where windows kindled the black bones of swingsets
in the distant housing, she'd return to herself

like letters flown back to a name.

II

Where is the hire for which my life was hired?
Oh vanity of vanities, desire!
—Christina Rosetti

The word alone is just as general as the word bread.
—Maurice Blanchot

Peridot

The mattress loved the explicit. She would find
two coins: the plum coin of blood
hatched in its navel, and the semen, blued
with some relative's
distorted permanence. These

she scrubbed into ink, blurring
the proof of their bodies before the surface blanched
below the snowy window. She closed her eyes.
A man would call from a National Poll;
a map would unfold before the mailbox. She preferred
the loss of a line to the presence of a wall.
The bedstains

shot under her lids. Her body
wooed them back, within
membranes, tea-colored membranes, as an exercise
in perspective, in keeping things.
"Choose your focal point," they addled.
It was the same scenery
but phosphorescent
and rude, as if she slaved and labored
in coupling. These

were the obdurate words, others' versions
of the covenant, "be fruitful and multiply," and worse,
what comes with age (which she foresaw)
the slow deflations, urine maps, what children
leave in the nest, what liberates the mind
from order—the obscure
peridot. She seeps

out of herself in spots, a true creator,
pregnantly, but not
rehearsed in the logic of lying

within bounds. O cradle of my soul, the crumbs
that Gretel scatters on the stumps are not
for her to find her way back, but for others.

Figures, Giacometti

What was flame has hardened into a single substance
and what was good has decreased in the wide air, pressing
bronze in a dream of attenuation
until what was restless took space
and moved without movement, like the body
I become before sleep, flinging
identity in a dark curve through peripheral trees;

but their stippled limbs took form and their long skulls
contracted with the stars until breathing
and leaning quietly, level with hills,
they thread their way into the spires of the city
seeking professions in the squares

then what seemed lonely was not lonely
or what was speaking was not speaking
and in the time it takes to recover from sleep
on a rainy morning, I pick my name up
in a mood for water

while the figures advance
on altars of gravity
grazing the atmosphere in the shadows of their shadows,
a man with an ear, a woman with a hairdo
coming and going from the usual offices, though they
could have said Egypt or Paradise any other day.

Sequence in Lime

Not something inside but a sound
placing limes by the window

as all spheres resemble the world
in a world of resemblances, a stream

of milk running across the trees
shines on the limes, forming

small green provinces. Then wind
tapes us in as quietly as moss. We are turning

cans and fenders into rust in the yards
and scrub in the umber ground.

Not so much sound as color
placing oranges by the curtains. At night

headlights spin down the road,
immaculate skaters in shining

in-air pulpits, violent under crystal
constellations you could touch. We remember

setting lemons in the bowl by the window
and changing angles until they rubbed the moon

and the way a child watered all the stones
in a garden, and we watched,

on our tongues, *as if*—
but the mind is a broken distance.

A Verdant Season

The morning's pylons
thatching a sea-green blind
or a white blind, thumbed with botany;

the locust tree, leafed and seedy
clinging to milk-clouds, morning-sick and fat
like a phalanx

between here and the blue;
the pressure of song
coiling in a room under lungs

like a hoof
an utterance
for ripe musicians in the pit

of breath
when wisdom
is hunger for the roots

of every hunger
and the wish to unearth the shapes
of early memory, a carapace

and glean of inner rooms
against a frieze of sills, a single
color between whites.

On the street, I hear a woman saying she named her kid
    DiAngelo.
Something uttered into June
is the reason for mouths.

Night Attendants

You attend a death, the body shipping off,
the tongue so far in it cups the language below,
and the night black again, its water immaculate.
Impossible to imagine loneliness so much

like some parody of pure light, and the skin
consumed after the soapings and the spoonings, naked
in the off-color fantasy, the tones of sleep
and decay, when sleep sighs over the body. Imagine

how the prodding figures will come with requiems, sheets,
their muscular hands roiling each rib
like a curious package. They'll fall through spheres,
those night attendants, dressed

in fluorescent funk from the stars,
waiting while we shape our prayers, holed
in this lyrical self-love. You say
grief is a request for compensation.

This hand cups this breast at night
because it has no other place to go.

Film Blanc

Even the atoms refract the future of winter:
a stiff bride to cement and sparrows.
Walking, I think "oh earth" for a sort of love
without referent. The mist is exact with breath, crossing
the bone-colored path like film-work,
and ice—the way ice is—
suckles the bark,

and Mary in the next door grass kneels
in her aqua reliquary, foolproof as the infinite.
Is there a happy ending without gain? The Daily Double,
acquisitions, atonements?
What does it mean to possess yourself, balancing
the heartbeat's interior things
with the sky's palette of naked paper towel, swollen

with precipitation, flocks, electric nerves?
Imagination colludes with birds, brooming
the apex of a roof. And now another couple
sleeps late through entire reels, all beautifully translated
into fence posts, poles, the month's
self-love, which cannot be other
than itself.

Surplus

The heart—
a canned tulip—
cannot bear itself. And the mind's light masonry
houses a crap shoot, waterlit, below
the level of the dark. Here is the C-note
slapped on the table's jade block,
the insufferable jukebox that keeps the outfit tapping
as long as anyone survives: in smoke,
war-issue tables and chairs, the pale-faced clock, the body's
motor of wounds. A veteran
lifts his beer like a feather. A light breeze
unpins the curtains on the moon, a threshing blade, to a song
that dabbles among their ears (lady, moon, and veteran),
below the level of the Good. Outside,
an air of nostalgia brushes the wheat, the landscape
rigged with pie sills and holly, the scene
carved out of a headboard like flowers—
or out of the head—
either with the crooked stalks of a battlefield in the moonlight, or,
in some parody of a perfectly normal town,
where loved ones lie sleeping, without
any sense of the world.

The Ample House

A cold spring, and the stiffened rain
tips the nerve endings of the elm
with silver. A coral fly-wing sticks

to the sill. And here, a movie's thin,
misused starlet unpins her laundry,
goes back to her ticking kettle. Or rather

the actress playing the misused starlet.
All day rain licks the trees into smooth
hides, mammalian and incidental,

like music in the afternoon, with excerpts
of tea and jelly. What I remember most:
the somber velvet sky of early dark,

a birth! as though it were my mind
and not the rain in the mirror, a field
of glass that reflects flesh, a woman

(my mother) inside the glass, her inconstant moods,
her reflection without the voice, as if
she had turned to matter behind the room

in a scrim, returned to the trees
in the picture of a window. Aren't we
always in that house, dumb

before the saucers, cups, and ironing,
before a pile of shirts with the sleeves
turned out, like the ones the young, movie star double

deposes in a heap? In and out
of ourselves with occasional daydreams,

going incognito around the house
that fascinates, discovering lapses
in a room, where space
opens in light blue. A child's room,

odored with baskets, papered and swept bare.
The lintels loom and distort
across fat garlands. Rain leans over the street;

water swills around windows, mailboxes, and flowers,
and curtains gleam
against the inner lamps. I suppose their stoves

are full of cakes, the bedrooms full
of love and abuse. *Talk to me, talk.*
But no one does. The woman in the mirror

goes home to her quiet forest.
        Rain licks the trees, recalling further
our watery origins: to start

in a puddle of sleep, to call it
the ravishing dark.

Custody

Morning is new self-absorption
hissed inward on the fixed fields
of skin and bone.

You stretch
in currents of light, non-light,
through morning's pale infusions

where I recognize the eye: a sleeping face
still skimmed in hyaline shade
beneath a patch of sun

that vectors knees and arms.
Approach the lift and fall
of breath lapped

in liquid sheets, the shock of rousing
to clean, recumbent clouds,
the warm relief

of undulating rays, buckled
across the sills and islands
where we dwell in smooth

delineaments of form,
new hypotheses of permanence
and home.

Theater of the World

Here are lamps,
a dictionary open to marginal slides, diagrams,
until all organic life seems aberrant:
compound leaves, the compound eyes of a fly,
the world of an iris where a compound moon
cuts up. So there is no harmony here.
Outside, autumn's incredible pieces just fall around
like orange jewelry from a woman's blue body,
but the leaves have no implications.

A student comes with her silence, her books,
her *Elements of Biology* forming a black and green
wonderland picture of whorled leaves.
Inside the whiteness is in raptures, like a voice
turning back in its silk. And shyly
she takes cues as I blunder
"words mean things"
and her eyes live for seconds

then return to a sitting room of their own pleasure,
touching the keys and latches
while the power of lamplight
takes room in other bodies.
Each word, glued with unending multiplications of the aberrant—
the odd leaf stalk with plenitude, with hairs,

and other strange things—the sewer's breath,
a chart of phrenology, the phylactery on a ten year old,
or a pier diminished from the eye.
In the non-fading eye we seem continually whole and open,
but in her room she is a decimal fraction of the light
bending over her hands.

III

So doth each tear
Which thee doth wear,
A globe, yea world, by that impression grow,
Till thy tears mixed with mine do overflow
This world . . .

—John Donne

Daughter of the Hangnail

i.
Freeman left me on the expressway
so I had to book it with the f_____g diapers. Lost,

I might add, like a tune from God.

What you don't see won't hurt you.
Flurries of pollen, exhaust, lines

connecting equal points of sunlight. Sound?
One had to let the sound out of her mouth

in order to become fully human:
equal parts water and flesh. The noise

like a glyph, the slap of shape
on air, the air

as paper. But the paper
tremulous. A little dismantling in the box

where the word severs—
flesh of my flesh,

the man yelling "mama" by the exit ramp.

ii.
I think of this as the city of heaven. Heaven

descending
in powdered form. So you take all the wings and larvae,

blue bottle flies, soapbugs, moths
and other species glued to the underside

of rudimentary flora in an empty lot. The vigorous weed
and gull body, chicory, dozens of washers

propelled to the gutters
in slivers of milk glass, discarded needles,

the treacherous sand,
the collapsed condom, terra infirma

of the dislocated barrel and loose-strife.

iii.
I'm nothing but a prop

in this fiery, fumous descent.
A pot on the stove, a kid by the pot.

You get a whiff of burning.
Foam and acrylic interlap

from the many little flares in town.
In the murmur of wheels,

in the rumor of gold,
in the gust of sunlight

under the sooty windows. The sooty—
well—

aren't these the windows, thousands
upon thousands of small black holes, like felt

taped to the brick? And when I return
the house is in flames

and the neighbors all testify against me.

iv.
Then ask, what is my name?
Daughter of flames, daughter

of lust and goading.
Daughter of grit—

the smeary lips,

ailanthus, fleas, and cereal.
Daughter of the hangnail, dubious

with hunger. A balancing act
between paint chips

and the slow leaves. Time.
Though in those days, one couldn't embark

on embarkations. "Stay put," is what I did,
or do. In the interchangeable months, stuck

on the gnatty carpet, dreaming of gentry.
A lawn paradise, carpetry

of spilled animals.

v.
What does "here" mean?
In the height of July, the sun

furring the asphalt
in the baker's resonance, the dry-cleaner's tack,

the butcher
stringing up pigs in the market place.

I'm nothing but a voice
in the sub-strata of history,

a sheet

I might have pressed with unequal attention
just as I've ironed a single blouse

maybe a thousand mornings

where you cannot hear me—
and you cannot be known, and I am not

you, and I know nothing of you, in these

unsolid canopies, this hum.
In these

thousands of mornings.

Blue Shift

The heart sinks like a stone, but shines
in the forested room. When you try to touch
the intact gleam, you lose the galaxy
the way children obliterate stars with their fingers.

And night after night, you inhale onyx,
bringing black oxygen to the occluded tongue
like a long reel of Theolonious Monk
when blue light, water, smoke

officiate; you spin across the sheared mountains,
the dutiful moons of your mother's life
while coal dust sinks on fir and meaning—
"break yourself over this music," and in bed

green scents permeate the open room
so you know who you are
as if you had built your wall
and stayed in the universe.

The closest thing to your mouth
is breath turning back in its damp swell,
loosened in the sheets like those clumsy
shadow lines of cloud: amorphous

animals, the fractured shapes you love
because you walked in the shadow her love made
until you walked in your own love. Mornings
her feet turn into pink fins

crenulated on the old linoleum.
In each step, she leaves her film
burning briefly in invisible prints
as if night coiled under the body

and fell on the dusty floor
where space accumulates, no matter
how often you ruminate a hand
toward her palpable skin.

A Small Business

We arrive at the other end of our bodies
in work clothes: no prayers
to be said over the envelopes
that fold the hours up with bits of spit.
One eyes nothing less than fury.
The dead letter files, postage stamps,
small, quixotic loves
stuck in a collection of photographs
and embossed violets on your desk.
How shall I say it?
We know our place. Egos, paper-thin,
tuck demurely,
leaving the doors open in apertures of self/soul
that cool on the window ledge
as we fall into fatnesses. The dust
on the bottom of a cup
spells the odor of a room (the fan
full of rain) while our co-workers
snarl over a meatloaf, through the tick
of a bulb, the closed-up air, the ledgers
and debris, the soft teeth of machinery,
the hackneyed paint. When the flies trip upward, small
as messages from our open mouths, we know
our houses are on fire.

Affliction

Imagine I had been a town
filled with unusual sorrow: a woman lived

in the shut box of her room, neighbors
left yardwork to lapsed wilderness, kitchens

blazed, knives
stumbled, the nights bloomed

in wakeful agony, though the residents
barely worried about the world—

they were like an island of fishers
who discover bodies in their water, only here

the bodies were mere reverberations. Fear
that bobbed to the surface in effigies, after months

of inexpression. And the town,
jittery and aloof, skipped routine,

leaving love and grief to battle through the streets, unchecked,
which led to overwhelming helplessness—or art—

a single cry in the folding light
amid notes to pick up the laundry, or money

for the slumped taxis. You know
I am talking about my body,

how hard it is to accept the disturbances, especially joy
in a season of fear. Outside

the wind groans, the sky groans, the sea, trucks
on the arteries, your beauty,

the singing birds
in their armchair of song.

Redshift

A fire hydrant, a lawn, a ball,
and the light sky

    layered like smell—

someone has painted their foundations blue, and exited
before the clap of footprints. An echo

without the shoe
in a flock of seedlings.

I have lost my ear for the weather. Is there anything
to remind me?

    In the light dusk

where the season's oily tulips rise like pickets
by a house. And almost visible—

the family, sipping beer and soup
in an orange alcove. Flat in their heat

like the color of dark bread
    (the imported kind)

that sailed from Poland
in somebody's rumpled coat. It was then

that a girl stepped toward nuptials, and the finite

passed through the infinite,
along

    the imperceptible history of this street.

Haven't the petals struck you as tongues?
The weather tuned to a very fine overlay,

a light sheet surrounding its own girth
where sound

     recedes, like a bell. In which

sound recedes.

My song is a monologue that begins
in this pearl of space.

As a bird dips its wings in a pool,
and a ball disappears

     over a roof,

and over the roof (imagine *this*)
love, petrification,

     immensities—

and over the roof
a fire.

Error, Which the Mind Admits

Owls flying close to the ground
could be a sign of despair.

A poor woodswoman reverberates in my ear
like a Russian nesting-doll in her socks and apron.

She hasn't a clue to her fathomless house. All night
we dream up motifs: bread, night birds,

breasts, a woman's heavy dishevelment, the leaves
lying on the quilt like lions

seeking invidious entries
over the sills. It's a good house/

bad neighborhood. Animals, who inhabit our rooms
have a disregard for system. We breathe in

urine from the yard, touched
with foragers, before

releasing darkness from the sky's
obverse surface, where I touch

the red fizzle of morning,
a torn field through glass.

Sometimes I talk of going inside, on a kind of journey.
Intead, I find repetition:

the obscurantist's logic, watermarks,
and the error of beauty.

Catskill

Though the eye was meandering the voice
sought bricks and red bridges
over ravines

strapped with girders and woodland (no, it went
too far down for that, needing to gasp,

then pivot
back to the light bodices of trees).

A forum of clouds
brushed over the houses, and a man there
slept for a hundred years. The birds

scooped over the quiet bed
where the land lost him, and he turned
to a mote in the fluid dark.

Then some of us were born
during the years of his sleep.
We put in some mock tudor,

some service men, some Bing Crosby
and Lassie in the hills;
until he woke to the hounds' red tongues

crossing a blue sky,
to the solid hunter in thermal wear,
to the reliquaries and water jugs

joining the broken heaps of coal and railroad effluvia
by the brown depot, to
the Catholic shelter and the Elks'

where rain had oozed through the lintels
and the white stones, the mountains
made of the same stones.

Where sleep had scummed his throat
were slips of a prior language, light
moving up a ladder

through foreign circuitry, a rule
the eye could not depend on
even if he forgot his country.

After Crosswords

Amazed by your "ilex" I watch you go, driving
into June's green mouth with a species
of holly from our county of grid, and grasses
whose names may be fathomed
with currencies of cash
or single-celled creepers of sub-kingdoms,
the phyla of phenomena. Here
is beauty, there, deities stuck in boxes
like forsaken planets and references, the flowers,

islands, and celebrities, a thick gulf
that opens in martial, opalescent seas, squares
with birthstones and presidents. You
drive into another world of objects:
hills, intimate with silence.
Is silence inside or outside the head?
Is it possible to peel
eternal questions from the alphabet,
plumbing clues for Gods, which lattice

"a mild oath" like errors
in history's dehiscent mouth? How lithe
my idol will look when he appears, spilling
from the fruits of my alphabet, curiously
jeweled in amethyst. And I without modesty
will get down on the floor
where he christens linoleum with his fleshy hide.
And lo! a cloven hoof: a scale of emotions

hums with the utmost intensity
when he spells synonyms
on my neck and down
to the instep of my thighs, the crux
of all phenomena. He offers lessons in sin—
"or is that singing," he replies? crudely

mixing "love" with the "larynx."
Let me tilt my question up to him:

Am I in the world, or is the world
in me? He sighs, "rephrase and redeem!"
or syllables thereof.
Love, it is wild, wild when you leave.

The Endless Self

The poet makes his appearance in a bored world . . .
Baudelaire

To displace the labors of memory
is a wild task. In the spring's
musty flavors of rebirth: like folding
damp gray towels back in the primordial regions

of my breast. Something like that—a feeling
you'd have to pull with pincers, extracting
feather from bone. An illusion of sorrow, perhaps,
like the beautiful green veils over a room,

impounding light with their opacity
through windows in the homes, when yards
bore their owners' casual surfaces
of earth and bird-marks; evenings,

after the winter's last white breath
and the nervousness of ravens pressing for food.
Inside, some perfect felicity: layer cakes,
half-visible wicks and TV's,

when the sound of the local shook
our shoddy watering holes. At night
an even greater blue wheeled out
in sudden shades of lapis. We drank,

half-severed from ourselves between
the threats of radiation. *We'd go down
with the bastards if they pushed the button*—
would the walls glow

or chemicals in the water take us first
with lymphatic fish and toxins? And who would care?

Weren't our parents all divorced and/or
remarried, mothers

 we loved and could not love,
like our bodies, the shapes crosshatched
in margins, a girl in fishnets and overalls.
I envisioned petticoats

rising to the surface of the lake
where an earlier woman lost herself. Instead,
they brought in goldfish. The fat, orange carp
flashed beneath a footbridge, stippled

with water-life. My friend
wanted "proletarian" to describe herself
through a dream of ill-heated rooms. She dieted
on rice and tea until she glowed, not just

to simulate deprivation, but to find
the one thin place she survived from.
I wanted a house on the edge of town, steam
pluming from manholes, a red and blue

windowbox, strays
who'd nibble the grass down to the stones. Still,
there would be terror in that order,
as today, when the cops beat a man for speeding,

and the mind turns on that violence: flights
ending in a blunt instrument, the earlier self
postmarked without promise of arrival,
time, place, the former mouth,

which leaves no imprint on my face. When the sky pends
from all four windows, I see pressed

through exhaustless expanse, an arc
which the bird flies into. But here

there is merely the length a child walks to the corner stop-sign.
And here, objects provide an illusion of depth—
and finally, the glass is all tromp l'oeil, still-portrait
of roof and glimmer. This last

is the worst. Light spars from within, sidereal
and sunless. We are non-existent
to each other, deciphering flux
in the cool heels of the room,

like sole-survivors, fixed up
with bread and butter.
It is here they inflict pain, the dogs
with slicked mustaches who sniff deception,

who would eat the bones out of the garden, gristled shanks
exposed in the frost, whatever clings:
the lost red fibers and flower seed
in any casual dirt. Is it harder to imagine joy

than suffering? To construct
a path out of the house
that closes winter in its deadpan light,
where the unopened odors of spring

tease with an action that hasn't formed?
Some days, the mind excludes
all but leaf, walk, weather, or the moon. Still,
anything that moves outside the body

is not indifferent.

Photo by Rose Slirzewski

Rebecca Reynolds is the Assistant Director of the undergradu-
ate honors program at Douglass College, the women's college
of Rutgers, The State University of New Jersey. Her undergrad-
uate study was at Vassar, and she has since completed an MA
in English at Rutgers, and an MFA in Creative Writing at the
University of Michigan

Mary Ruefle is the author of four collections of poetry, most
recently *The Adamant*, co-winner of the Iowa Poetry Prize; and
Cold Pluto, from Carnegie Mellon University Press. She teaches
at Vermont College.